ESSENTIAL MONEY SKILLS FOR TEENS

Understanding the basics of money, financial planning, a healthy credit history, growing wealth and taxes.

by
SAVANNAH UWOM

TABLE OF CONTENTS

Introduction

Welcome to an adventure into the world of financial empowerment that goes beyond the typical bounds of teenagers. You are about to go on a life-changing journey that will not only reshape your current situation but also set the groundwork for a stable financial future as soon as you pick up this book.

Knowing the ins and outs of money is like having superpowers in the fast-paced fabric of modern life. The secret to releasing such power is to read "Essential Money Skills for Teens". This is not a book on intricate financial theories or secret investing methods. Rather, it's a useful and approachable manual catered to the particular requirements of teenagers.

We will explore the foundational elements of personal finance chapter by chapter. This book serves as your guide as you navigate the confusing world of online banking and budgeting, helping you grasp the fundamentals of both. It acknowledges the difficulties faced by youngsters in a time of unparalleled consumerism and information access. We'll deconstruct financial jargon as we go over subjects like earning, saving, and investing.

Why is this information important to you as a modern-day teenager? Empowerment is the solution.

When handled properly, money may be a tool to help you achieve your goals and objectives. It's important to make decisions that are in line with your ideals and aspirations rather than just focusing on gaining cash.

You'll learn the value of setting financial goals, how to make wise spending choices, and how to develop a savings attitude as we travel together. We'll explore the fascinating world of entrepreneurship, negotiate the credit world, and solve the tax mysteries.

Beyond its usefulness, this book seeks to foster a sense of financial assurance. Money can be a source of empowerment and independence rather than a source of worry or uncertainty. You'll learn things that go beyond the printed word thanks to applicable anecdotes, interactive exercises, and real-world situations.

"Essential Money Skills for Teens" is an investment in your future self, not just a manual. Together, let's set out on this adventure, which will provide you the information and abilities to confidently and purposefully traverse the financial terrain. The beginning of your financial future is today.

CHAPTER 1 :UNDERSTANDING MONEY BASICS

Learning the fundamentals of money is like learning a universal language that controls our lives' economic environments. This chapter takes us on an exploration of the complexities surrounding money, its place in society, and the basic ideas that guide our financial dealings.

In essence, money is a medium of trade that permits the intricate network of transactions that characterizes modern economies, not just bits of paper or digital figures on a screen. It functions as a unit of account, giving the worth of goods and services a standard measurement. Understanding money better reveals that it is a social construct that impacts our daily lives and influences our decisions, transcending its material form.

The faith we have in money determines its value. The value of any legal currency, be it a dollar bill, euro, or something else entirely, comes from the trust that its holders place in its ability to hold onto its value and conduct business. This trust serves as the foundation for the complex financial systems that characterize our globalized world and is essential to stable economies.

Understanding the concept of inflation is crucial as we navigate the world of personal finance. Over time, inflation, or the steady rise in the average price of goods and services, reduces the purchasing power of money. It is essential to comprehend this phenomenon since it affects long-term financial planning and decision-making. It challenges us to think about the true worth of money in the face of shifting economic conditions, in addition to its face value.

As essential components of the financial system, banks are essential to the production and flow of money. By serving as middlemen and taking deposits and making loans, they efficiently transfer money from savers to borrowers. Fractional reserve banking, in which banks retain only a portion of their deposits in reserve so they can lend out the remainder and increase the money supply, is fundamental to this process. The foundation of contemporary banking systems, this process both promotes economic expansion and presents difficulties, such as the possibility of financial crises.

The evolution of money in the digital era goes beyond paper money. Digital currencies and online transactions, which serve as electronic money, are becoming more and more common. With the emergence of decentralized currencies like Bitcoin and Ethereum, cryptocurrencies have cast doubt on conventional ideas of money and the direction of finance. Although these advances create new opportunities, they also bring with them complexity and uncertainty, which influence how money is changing.

Part of the economic fabric that keeps our money secure and sound are the financial institutions. As guardians of monetary policy, central banks control the money supply and interest rates to preserve stability in the economy. Individuals have access to a variety of financial options thanks to the services offered by commercial banks, credit unions, and other financial institutions. These services vary from savings accounts to mortgages.

Recognizing the economic factors that influence the value of money is another aspect of understanding it. Currency prices fluctuate due to supply and demand dynamics affected by government policies, geopolitical events, and technological breakthroughs. Because of the interdependence of the world economy, exchange rates and the relative value of one currency relative to another play a significant role in international trade and finance.

Understanding the cultural and historical influences on how we view money is crucial to understanding the fundamentals of money. Throughout human history, money has existed in many forms and has changed from barter systems to complex financial instruments. Cultural influences shape our values and behaviors about earning, spending, and saving money, as well as our attitudes toward money.

What is Money?

Fundamentally, money is a medium of exchange that makes economic system transactions easier. It functions as a store of value, enabling people to accumulate and transfer purchasing power over time, as well as a unit of account, giving people a standard way to measure the value of products and services.

Over the ages, the idea of money has changed to meet the shifting demands of various communities. Barter systems, which involved the direct exchange of commodities and services, were common in the past. But barter's drawbacks, like the requirement for both parties to desire what the other has such as the double coincidence of wants led to the creation of money as a middleman.

There are many different physical and digital forms of modern money. Coins and banknotes are examples of tangible, internationally recognized money. In the digital age, digital currency numbers displayed on displays and in electronic databases have proliferated. A relatively recent invention, cryptocurrencies use decentralized blockchain technology to offer digital money that is not governed by conventional financial institutions.

People's confidence and trust in money is the foundation of its worth. The idea that money has value and can be traded for goods and services underpins all forms of money, including decentralized cryptocurrencies and government-issued money. Stable financial institutions and economies are built on this trust.

In a nutshell, money is a social construct that acts as a store of value, a medium of exchange, and a unit of account to enable economic transactions. Its development is a reflection of human societies' dynamic character and their constant search for more effective and efficient ways to engage in trade and commerce.

Type of money

In all of its manifestations, money functions as a store of value, a unit of account, and a medium of exchange. Based on their issuance, representation, and materiality, different forms of money can be grouped. Let's examine the various types of money:

Commodity Money:

Commodity money is similar to owning a valuable trading card that has a consensus value of a specific sum. What if you could use rare Pokémon cards for purchases as well as for entertaining battles? That is the fundamental concept of commodity money.

Commodity money in the past included items like gold and silver. These were unique because, similar to a glittering Pokémon card, they were valuable in and of themselves. Put another way, exchanging a gold coin for something was like telling someone, "I'm giving you this because it's worth a certain amount of something valuable."

Each card has a unique worth, similar to trading your rarest cards with pals. But consider a scenario in which every member of your group felt that a particular card was extremely special and could be used to purchase games or food. Commodity money operated in this way: it had inherent value and was seen as reliable due to its scarcity and utility. Even if we don't directly use gold or silver to purchase goods today, comprehending commodity money enables us to grasp how various items have served as "special cards" to exchange for goods throughout history.

Representative Money:

Representative money functions similarly to a special coupon that guarantees you a specific amount of precious metals like silver or gold. Let's say you have a concert ticket; while the ticket doesn't actually reflect the music, it does represent your entitlement to attend the performance. Similar principles apply to representative money, which is a form of currency that is not intrinsically valuable but rather symbolizes a claim to something of worth.

Representative money, which could be traded for a set quantity of precious metals like gold or silver, was utilized in the past. Imagine having a paper note that says, "You can trade this for a piece of gold." That's how it feels. This system contributed to the convenience of dealing and purchasing.

Our primary type of money today is fiat money, which is similar to representational money. Fiat money is valuable because people believe it can be used to purchase goods and services, not because it has intrinsic value. Hence, your regular money functions as a kind of unique ticket that signifies its value, streamlining transactions and purchases in the contemporary world.

Flat Money:

We utilize fiat money on a daily basis, and it works somewhat like magic! Fiat money lacks intrinsic value, as opposed to coins composed of precious metals or paper linked to anything significant. Rather, its value stems from what the government declares.

Let's say you are playing a game and everyone knows that numbers on a screen or colorful pieces of paper indicate worth. Fiat money is that! These bits of paper or digital numbers become legal tender when they are declared by the government, which functions something like the referee in our game. Because everyone believes they have value, we can use them to purchase goods.

Therefore, you are utilizing fiat money when you exchange your allowance for a video game or spend cash to pay for food. Everything is predicated on faith and the conviction that these bits of paper or digital data have value in the eyes of others. Our daily interactions are facilitated by a kind of shared knowledge that makes it easier for you to negotiate the world of buying and selling in day-to-day transactions.

Cryptocurrency:

Let's dissect cryptocurrency, such as Bitcoin and Ethereum, which may appear to be magical online cash. Consider conventional money as coins or paper that a government issues. On the other hand, cryptocurrency is digital and runs on a system known as blockchain.

Imagine a massive, distributed digital ledger, a fancy term for an accounting system that is shared by a number of computers on a network. A blockchain is created when a bitcoin transaction is made and is recorded in a block that is linked to previous blocks, thus the name "blockchain."

Why is it unique? Cryptocurrencies are not governed by a single organization, such as a bank or government. Instead, to safeguard transactions, they use intricate arithmetic and computer code. Because the records are decentralized, nobody can alter them.

Adolescents consider it autonomous, transparent, and secure digital currency. Without using a regular bank, anyone can use cryptocurrencies to send money overseas, make investments, and purchase items. It's similar to having your own digital wallet, giving you access to new opportunities in the dynamic world of money.

Commercial Bank Money (Checkable Deposits):

Checkable deposits from commercial banks, in particular, are like your financial command center. Money deposited in a bank is not left there idle. Rather, it is included into what is referred to as commercial bank currency. Consider it as your digital wallet, which you may access using debit cards, credit cards, and online transactions.

The truth is that when you put money into a bank account—whether it be your earnings or allowance—you are effectively contributing to the overall amount of money that the bank is managing. This money is digitally recorded in your account; it does not exist as actual notes and coins.

You are now using this digital money when you pay for that delicious snack or the newest video game with your debit card. It's very convenient because all you need to carry is a piece of plastic or your smartphone instead of a bunch of cash.

Therefore, the electronic version of your money that is readily available for use in daily transactions is represented by your checkable deposits. It's similar to having a simple and safe portal where you can swipe or click to manage your finances, make purchases, and handle anything related to money.

Central Bank Money

The engine that powers our financial system, central bank money, is like the superpower of money. Think of it as the captain of the financial team, with electronic reserves and hard currency (coins and banknotes) as the two main players.

First, there is actual cash that you can handle and spend. Are those the bills that are in your wallet? That is actual money from the central bank. It is constantly prepared for action, much like the rock star of money.

The electronic side comes next. Money deposited in a bank is not left there. It is used. With the central bank, the bank maintains a computerized record of it as electronic reserves. It's similar to having a covert agent making sure your money is secure behind closed doors.

Physical cash and electronic reserves, when combined, constitute central bank money and serve as the foundation of our financial system. To maintain the equilibrium of our economy, the central bank supervises and controls this money like a sage guardian. You are therefore a participant in the central bank money adventure whether you pay with cash or your card!

The Value of Currency

The worth of money is not limited by the paper or metal on which it is printed. By exploring this idea, we reveal the complex web that intertwines society structures, economic theories, and personal goals. Money is more than just a means of transaction; it's also a symbol of trust, worth, and the complex interplay between supply and demand.

Fundamentally, money serves as a bridge that links people in the huge market for goods and services, facilitating transactions. The fact that human ingenuity was able to develop a system that allowed us to go beyond barter and create a standardized unit of value that is independent of the constraints of direct exchange is a monument to that.

The concepts of supply and demand in economics are closely related to the value of money. The relationship between these two basic forces determines how much money is worth in the market. The value of a currency tends to increase as demand outpaces supply. On the other hand, depreciation may result from excess supply. Modern economies revolve around this fragile equilibrium, which affects everything from the cost of living to commodity prices.

Nevertheless, economic forces do not affect the value of currency alone. It reflects the confidence and trust of society. A currency's ability to remain stable is closely related to the trust that people and organizations have in the system that controls it. Through the implementation of prudent fiscal policies, the control of inflation, and the maintenance of the general stability of the economic environment, governments, central banks, and financial institutions play a crucial role in upholding this trust.

In the past, money has come in all shapes and sizes, including shells, pearls, and precious metals. The majority of currencies in use today are fiat and digital. The change from paper money to digital money emphasizes how our financial system is always changing. Cryptocurrencies and other digital currencies add new elements to the value equation by highlighting transparency, security, and decentralization.

Money has significant cultural and psychological significance in addition to its economic and technological aspects. It represents a society's overall ideals and ideas. The pictures, emblems, and historical people that adorn banknotes convey a narrative about the identity, history, and goals of a country. Money takes on the role of a vessel carrying the spirit of a community, encouraging harmony and a sense of purpose.

Furthermore, money has a very personal meaning. For individuals, it symbolizes not only their purchasing power but also the result of their labor, expertise, and experience. Earning money is a product of hard work and imagination, and one's decision about how to spend or preserve it is a reflection of their own priorities and objectives.

Currency values in the international society we live in are intertwined. Currency fluctuations in one nation can have an effect on international trade, investments, and geopolitical dynamics outside national boundaries. It is imperative that both individuals and politicians comprehend this interconnection, as it influences global financial decision-making and determines economic policies.

Introduction to Banking

A cornerstone in the complex web of contemporary finance, banking is a multidimensional organization that is essential to determining the direction of the economy. As we explore the world of banking, remember that it is more than simply a place to keep money; it is a dynamic force that affects the movement of capital, makes transactions easier, and promotes economic expansion.

In its most basic form, banking serves as a bridge that connects those with excess money to those who require capital. The origins of banking can be seen throughout human history, progressing from basic barter systems to the complex financial organizations that currently support the world economy.

The acceptance of deposits is one of the core duties of a bank. When people put their trust in a bank, they are entering into a partnership based on dependability and trust. The foundation of banks' economic operations is the careful balancing act they do while providing loans and earning interest on these deposits.

Banks do more than only accept deposits; they also operate as the keepers of financial records. Banks offer checking and savings accounts that give customers a safe location to keep their money and easy access for regular transactions. Because of their ease of use and guarantee of security, banks become essential parts of our everyday existence.

The banking industry has seen a radical change in the digital age. The modern banking experience is now synonymous with electronic transactions, smartphone apps, and online banking. In addition to making account holders' lives easier, this evolution puts established banking models under pressure to change in response to a world that is becoming more interconnected.

Because of their varied functions and customer base, banks are not homogenous entities. The most well-known banks to the general public, commercial banks offer both individuals and companies a variety of services. Investment banks assist companies in raising finance through the sale of stocks and bonds, with an emphasis on the capital markets. In order to preserve economic stability, central banks which frequently function at the national level play a crucial role in monetary policy by controlling the money supply and interest rates.

The foundation of banking is the idea of interest, which powers financial transactions. People pay interest when they borrow money in exchange for the ability to use someone else's money. On the other hand, people who make deposits into savings accounts receive interest as payment for letting the bank use their money for lending.

The impact of banking on the economy is further heightened with the introduction of the fractional reserve system. By lending out a fraction of the deposits they own, banks are able to create fresh money in the form of loans thanks to this method. This mechanism adds risk and complexity to the financial system even as it stimulates economic growth by providing capital for investment.

History has demonstrated that banks are not impervious to crises. Financial institutions may encounter difficulties like liquidity crises or economic downturns. Maintaining the stability and integrity of the banking system makes smart management, regulation, and oversight crucial.

The idea of socially conscious banking has gained popularity recently. This strategy encourages banks to think about the larger effects of their activities on society and the environment by emphasizing moral and sustainable practices. The growing preference for values-aligned banking among consumers forces financial companies to embrace socially responsible and transparent operations.

The banking industry is a complex web that is intertwined across our whole economic existence. Banking has an impact on both the general direction of economies and our daily lives, from the fundamentals of deposit taking to the intricacies of international financial markets. Understanding the dynamics, roles, and changing nature of banking is crucial for navigating this complex environment and is not just a financial talent; it also holds the key to deciphering the larger mysteries of the contemporary world. The trip into banking, whether you're depositing your first paycheck or thinking about investing ideas, is a voyage of financial literacy that equips people to confidently and intelligently navigate the currents of the global economy.

CHAPTER 2: BUDGETING FOR TEENS

Budgeting for teenagers is a dynamic financial plan that extends beyond income and expenses. This guide provides teens with the necessary tools to make deliberate and well-informed financial decisions by navigating the complex world of personal finance. Teens' budgets are essentially individual plans that describe their income, expenses, and savings.

Finding many sources of income, such as allowances, earnings from a part-time work, or cash gifts, is essential to comprehending the fundamentals of budgeting. Teens that take this first step are better able to understand their income. Making a fixed and variable spending category list is the next important step. While variable expenses, like leisure or personal things, fluctuate, fixed expenses, such subscriptions or school-related costs, are constant.

Financial goal-setting is a necessary step in budget creation. The aforementioned objectives function as a catalyst, encouraging teenagers to contemplate their financial aspirations. These goals influence the process of budgeting, whether it's setting aside money for a certain item, giving to a charity, or creating an emergency fund.

Following the creation of a budget makes spending tracking crucial. All spending activities, regardless of amount, must be routinely recorded. Teens are better able to maintain accountability and make necessary modifications to stay within their budgetary constraints when they regularly assess their spending. It is a talent that promotes balance and flexibility to change expenditures in one area to make room for another.

The budget of a teen must include setting financial goals. Long-term objectives like budgeting for college fees or short-term ones like saving for a new device can both be achieved. It is ensured that teenagers actively pursue their ambitions by including monies in the budget to help them.

Budgeting is essentially a life-changing tool for teenagers. A goal-oriented mindset is promoted, financial awareness is developed, decision-making abilities are sharpened, and flexibility is ingrained. Teens can manage their current financial environment and build a strong foundation for future financial success and independence by learning the art of budgeting early on.

Creating Your First Budget

- **Identify Income Sources:** Make a list of every source of income you have. This can include earnings from part-time work, babysitting duties, or allowances. Comprehending your sources of money is the initial stage towards proficient budgeting.

- **List Your Expenses:** List all of your recurring expenses in detail. Items such as personal belongings, entertainment, and school supplies may fall under this category. Sort them into two categories: variable (fluctuating) and fixed (unchanging).

- **Set Financial Goals:** Think about the goals you have for your finances. It could be putting money aside for a certain purchase, creating an emergency fund, or making a charitable donation. Your budgetary selections will be guided by your aims.

Tracking Your Expenses

After creating a budget, the following action is to monitor your expenditures. This aids in figuring out where your money is going and where adjustments might be made. To keep track of your everyday spending, use a spreadsheet, a budgeting tool, or even a plain notebook.

Tips for Tracking Expenses:

- **Be Consistent:** Keep track of all your expenses, no matter how tiny. This includes the impulsive app you downloaded or the hasty snack you grabbed from the school vending machine.

- **Review Regularly:** Every week, set aside some time to analyze your expenditures. You can stay accountable and make necessary adjustments with the support of this habit.
- **Adjust as Necessary:** Be prepared to make adjustments in other areas to stay under your budget if you find that you are overspending in one area. Finding a balance that suits you is the key.

Setting Financial Goals

Your budget is a tool to help you reach your financial objectives, not merely a way to keep track of your spending. Your budget can be adjusted to support your goals, whether they are long-term college fees, saving for a new device, or organizing a trip with friends.

Steps to Set and Achieve Financial Goals:

1. **Define Your Goals:** Clearly articulate what you want to achieve. This could be short-term (buying a new phone) or long-term (saving for college).
2. **Assign Costs:** Estimate how much money each goal will require. Breaking down large goals into

smaller, manageable parts makes them more achievable.

3. **Allocate Funds:** Make changes to your budget to set aside money for your objectives. This guarantees that you are actively pursuing your top priorities.

Benefits of Budgeting for Teens

Beyond just managing money directly, budgeting has several advantages for teenagers. These are the main benefits.:

1. **Financial Awareness:** Making a budget helps people become more conscious of their financial condition. Teens grow increasingly aware of their earnings, outlays, and general spending patterns. This heightened awareness creates the foundation for prudent money management.

2. **Goal-Oriented Mindset:** Budgeting makes financial goal-setting and achievement second nature. Teens acquire the ability to define and work toward goals, whether they are long-term (like saving money for college) or short-term (like buying a new device). A sense of purpose and achievement is fostered by this goal-oriented mindset.

3. **Decision-Making Skills:** Budgeting encourages teens to make intentional decisions about their money. Whether it's allocating funds for entertainment, savings, or necessities, the process instills a thoughtful approach to financial choices. This skill set proves invaluable as teens transition into adulthood.
4. **Adaptability:** Setting up a budget gives teenagers the flexibility to adjust when things change. Teens may make well-informed revisions to their financial plans with the skills they gain through budgeting, regardless of unforeseen expenses or changes in income. One essential component of financial resilience is this flexibility.
5. **Responsibility and Accountability:** One develops a sense of accountability for their financial well-being through budget management. The realization that financial actions have repercussions helps teens develop a stronger sense of responsibility. Their basic knowledge equips kids for the more significant financial obligations that come with growing up.
6. **Savings Habit:** Budgeting encourages the development of a savings habit. Allocating funds specifically for savings goals, whether for emergencies or future endeavors, establishes a pattern of disciplined saving. This habit becomes a powerful tool for building financial security over time.

7. **Financial Independence:** Teens set out on a path to financial independence through budgeting. They become more self-assured and proficient money managers, which lessens their dependency on outside funding sources. This early sense of self-sufficiency establishes the foundation for future prosperity.
8. **Life Skills Development:** Budgeting is a complete life skill, not just something to do with money. Adolescents acquire time management, planning, and organizing abilities. These abilities are beneficial to them in many areas of their lives and go beyond personal money.

CHAPTER 3: EARNING AND SAVING

The chapters on earning and saving serve as cornerstones of financial stability and empowerment in the maze of personal finance. For teenagers, these ideas represent the start of a path toward financial independence and appropriate money management, not just saving pennies for later or piling them up in a piggy bank.

Teenagers can make money in ways other than through part-time work or allowances. It's about realizing your abilities, your interests, and the special chances that are all around you. This chapter encourages you to investigate the several avenues for earning money and to consider innovative ways to transform your interests into profitable endeavors. The options are endless, whether it's providing services to nearby residents, making use of internet resources, or developing a hobby into a side gig.

Comprehending the worth of money acquired is equally essential. You may not make a lot of money as an adolescent, but the teachings in this chapter go well beyond that. It's about developing a work ethic and sense of responsibility that will benefit you in all of your future undertakings, and it's about understanding the time and effort required to earn every dime.

Saving money is a skill that changes your perspective on money and is frequently regarded as a financial superpower. Setting aside money isn't the only thing to do; it's a way of thinking and a deliberate choice to give future needs and objectives top priority. This chapter walks you through the art of saving, stressing the value of establishing realistic savings objectives. The method is always the same when saving money for a new device, future schooling costs, or a dream trip: a methodical and disciplined approach to putting money aside.

The process of creating your first savings plan is thrilling. It entails determining your long- and short-term financial goals, comprehending emergency fund concepts, and putting together a reasonable savings schedule. You'll experience the liberating sensation of financial control as you go on your journey, knowing that you have the resources to deal with unforeseen costs and pursue your goals.

The digital era has completely changed the way we handle our finances, and this chapter explains how you may use technology to improve your ability to earn and save. You'll learn about the security and ease of handling your money virtually, from the fundamentals of internet banking to the usage of digital payment options. It is crucial to comprehend the nuances of internet security to make sure that, in an increasingly linked world, your hard-earned money is safe.

Learning about earning and saving will teach you life lessons in addition to financial ones. Your financial management will help you develop discipline in all facets of your life, including your relationships with others and your academic endeavors. No matter how little the decision you make now, it sets the stage for success and financial security down the road.

Earning and saving money as a teenager is, in essence, a chapter in your life's narrative rather than just a chapter in a book. It's about taking charge of your financial story, accepting responsibility, and realizing your worth. Your financial path will include twists and turns, and the skills you learn here will act as a compass to help you navigate with confidence and purpose.

Exploring Ways to Earn Money

Exploring Ways to Earn Money provides an introduction to the exciting world of revenue production for teenagers in the context of personal finance. This chapter aims to expand your view of the plethora of options accessible to you, beyond the conventional boundaries of part-time work. It's an investigation into finding your interests, skills, and entrepreneurial spirit in addition to finding ways to make money.

Earning money as a teenager provides a chance for skill development and self-discovery in addition to financial gain. A potential area of investigation is the gig economy, a digital environment that has broadened the scope of work opportunities for people of all ages. You may make money doing freelance work in fields like writing, digital marketing, and graphic design by using platforms like these.

And don't forget about the influence of social media. Content creation is made possible by so many platforms in an era where connectivity is crucial. Regardless of your interests in fashion, gaming, or imparting knowledge, these platforms can serve as both venues for your own expression and possible sources of cash through collaborations, sponsorships, or advertising.

Investigating the realm of internet surveys and market research is an additional worthwhile endeavor. Businesses are keen to learn about the perspectives of the younger generation, and answering surveys can be a simple way to supplement your income. Even though it might not make you wealthy right away, it's an easy and convenient approach to start earning money.

Take into account local options in your community in addition to those found online. Traditional yet dependable ways to make money include babysitting, pet sitting, lawn care, and tutoring. In addition to offering cash benefits, these activities foster important life skills including communication, time management, and responsibility.

Teenagers are finding greater acceptance in the field of entrepreneurship, which is often associated with adults. Starting a small business, selling handcrafted goods, or providing a special community service are all examples of how entrepreneurship lets you use your imagination and initiative. From determining a market niche to drafting a basic business plan, this chapter walks you through the process of turning an idea into a successful business enterprise.

Another option to think about is volunteering, which offers possible networking opportunities in addition to the intrinsic gratification of doing good deeds. Participating in volunteer work can lead to opportunities for internships or part-time work, and the skills you acquire from charitable work can improve your resume and set you apart in the future.

This chapter emphasizes the importance of balance, which is important. Finding financial independence is a noble goal, but it's important to balance employment and other responsibilities in life. Teenage years are a time for self-discovery and exploration; therefore, your financial goals should support rather than interfere with your personal and intellectual development.

The Art of Saving: A Teen's Guide

Saving is more than just being frugal; it's a skill that creates a web of stability, adaptability, and opportunities for the future. Savings is a fundamental aspect of personal finance, encompassing more than just setting aside a percentage of your income. It's an intentional and thoughtful deed, an investment in your own destiny.

Fundamentally, saving is about developing a mindset of readiness and independence rather than just amassing wealth. The draw of instant gratification can be too strong in the daily rush of things. The newest technology, chic attire, or alluring events might entice us, drawing us away from the skill of saving money. However, the real beauty of saving is shown when one resists these desires.

Saving is a deliberate decision to put off short-term gratification in favor of long-term security. It is a type of delayed gratification. It calls for discipline, which in an age of rapid texting and on-demand services, may appear archaic. However, the basis for financial well-being is precisely this discipline.

A crucial first step in becoming an expert saver is establishing specific, achievable objectives. Having a goal for your savings, be it a down payment for a future home, an emergency fund, or a dream vacation, gives you focus and inspiration. Objectives serve as beacons, directing your financial choices and giving your saving regimen a feeling of direction.

The ability to distinguish between requirements and wants is another aspect of the art of conserving. It's critical to discern between necessities and discretionary spending in a consumer-driven world. By establishing a budget that reflects your values, you can make sure that money is spent wisely and that saving becomes an essential component of your overall financial strategy.

Embracing frugality is another brushstroke in the canvas of saving. This promotes a deliberate approach to spending rather than advocating a life of deprivation. Finding deals, reusing things, and appreciating the simplicity of life are all aspects of a thrifty way of living that add to the masterwork of saving.

Here's when automating your finances becomes an artistic endeavor. Consistency is ensured by setting up automatic transfers from your checking to savings account. It makes saving ingrained in your financial routine and eliminates the temptation to spend money that could be saved. Automation makes saving appear natural and essential, much like a well-practiced brushstroke on your financial canvas.

The unforeseen turns and turns of life do not exclude the skill of saving. Even the most careful financial plans can be derailed by emergencies, whether they are small setbacks or significant calamities. A strong savings plan foresees these unanticipated circumstances, acting as a safety net to lessen the blow of life's uncertainties.

Furthermore, saving is an art that involves more than just the person; it's a collective duty. Educating the next generation about the value of saving is an investment in the financial stability of the community. By educating others about the value of saving, we foster a resilient and financially literate culture that permeates the entire community.

In summary, saving is a craft that is constantly evolving; it is a canvas that is intentionally, systematically, and purposefully painted. It is a continuous process that changes based on your objectives, situation, and dreams. By developing this ability, you not only safeguard your financial future but also add to a story of empowerment and resilience. The skill of saving shows that you have the power to create a safer and more promising future.

Building Your First Savings Plan

The first step toward reaching your goals and achieving financial stability is creating your first savings plan. By giving your money structure, direction, and a roadmap, a savings plan gives you the power to take charge of your financial future. This is a guide to assist you in creating a customized and successful savings plan.

Understanding Your Finances

Prior to creating a savings plan, evaluate your financial status. Compute your monthly earnings, enumerate your customary outlays, and pinpoint places where you might reduce or maximize your expenditures. Realistic savings targets are based on this clarity.

Setting Clear Goals

Establish your long- and short-term financial goals. Long-term objectives can include retirement, housing, or education savings; short-term objectives might be setting up an emergency fund or saving for a particular purchase. Your savings efforts will be motivated and guided by well-defined goals.

Emergency Fund: Your Financial Safety Net

Prioritize building an emergency fund as a crucial aspect of your savings plan. Aim for three to six months' worth of living expenses. This fund acts as a safety net during unexpected financial challenges, providing peace of mind and preventing the need to dip into other savings for unforeseen expenses.

Creating a Budget

Creating a savings plan requires creating a budget. Before creating a budget for discretionary expenditure, set aside a percentage of your salary for savings. Your financial habit will become non-negotiable when you adopt this rigorous method to saving.

Choosing the Right Savings Accounts

Explore different types of savings accounts to find the one that aligns with your goals. Consider factors such as interest rates, accessibility, and any associated fees. Having a separate savings account dedicated to each goal can help you track progress more effectively.

Automating Your Savings

Set up automatic transfers from your checking to your savings account. Automation instills consistency, eliminating the need for manual transfers and reducing the temptation to skip saving in a particular month. Treat your savings contributions as non-negotiable commitments.

Tracking Your Progress

Regularly review your savings plan and track your progress toward each goal. Adjust your plan if needed, considering changes in income, expenses, or the timeline for your goals. Celebrate milestones to stay motivated on your financial journey.

Adjusting for Life Changes

Because life is dynamic, your savings strategy should also be flexible. Be ready to modify your plan in response to any changes in your goals, employment status, or other circumstances. Being adaptable guarantees that your savings plan stays appropriate for your changing situation.

Seeking Professional Advice

If you have specific financial goals or concerns, consider seeking advice from a financial advisor. They can provide tailored guidance based on your unique circumstances, helping you refine your savings plan and make informed decisions.

Cultivating a Savings Mindset

Beyond the numbers, developing a savings mindset entails realizing the benefits of regular saving over time, learning to separate requirements from wants, and accepting the value of postponing gratification. It's about seeing saving as an effective tool for reaching your goals rather than as a limitation.

Creating your first savings plan is a critical step in gaining financial autonomy. It puts you in a confident position to face life's uncertainties and work toward the future you want. As you set out on this path, keep in mind that every dollar you put into savings brings you one step closer to reaching your goals and ensuring your financial security.

CHAPTER 4: NAVIGATING THE DIGITAL WORLD OF FINANCE

Online Banking Basics

The emergence of online banking has revolutionized personal finance, with people managing their finances in a way that is always changing. "Online Banking Basics" is a doorway to ease, accessibility, and improved financial control—it's more than just a facet of contemporary banking.

Accepting the Digital Era

The conventional perception of banking, which included physical branches and long lines, has drastically changed. The modern solution to the demand for speed and efficiency in financial transactions is online banking. Fundamentally, it's about managing and accessing different financial services online from the convenience of your computer or mobile device.

Convenience and Accessibility

The unparalleled accessibility that internet banking provides is one of its main benefits. Users are no longer restricted by physical locations or banking hours and can check account balances, transfer money, and pay bills whenever and wherever they choose. The flexibility to transact financial business outside of regular business hours offers a degree of convenience that fits in well with the busy schedules of today's teenagers.

How to Use the Virtual Branch

By logging into your online banking platform, you can access a 24/7 virtual branch. An overview of your account balances, recent activities, and pending payments are usually shown on the dashboard. The interface is made to be easy to use, with menus that make it simple to access different features and services.

Easily Transferring Money

Teens can easily transfer money with the use of online banking. The process is simple and can frequently be finished in a matter of minutes, regardless of whether you're managing your personal accounts across many banks or sending money to friends or relatives. An previously unthinkable sensation of control over your cash is fostered by this immediacy.

Bill Payment Made Simple

The days of writing checks and mailing bills are long gone. Teens can effectively manage their financial obligations by using online banking. With just a few clicks, you can set up regular payments or make one-time payments for anything from utility bills to

41

subscription services. This lowers the possibility of missing deadlines in addition to saving time.

Increased Security Protocols

In the digital age, security is of utmost importance, particularly with regard to financial activities. Advanced security protections are built into online banking platforms to protect your data. These frequently consist of encryption, real-time fraud monitoring, and multi-factor authentication. Being aware of and making use of these security precautions is crucial to safely navigate the world of online banking.

Tools for Budgeting and Monitoring

Online banking offers options for budgeting and spending trend tracking in addition to standard transaction services. Teens have access to goal-setting tools, expense classification, and notifications for strange account behavior. People who take a proactive approach to money management are better equipped to make educated decisions and develop appropriate financial habits at a young age.

Accepting Financial Knowledge

Including internet banking in your daily financial routine is a path toward financial literacy, not just about making transactions. Gaining the ability to traverse the virtual financial landscape is the first step toward becoming financially independent and knowledgeable in general.

Every contact, from examining transaction history to reading electronic statements, adds to a comprehensive understanding of personal finance.

Online banking represents a fundamental change in how we view and deal with money, not just a technical innovation. Teens who embrace the fundamentals of internet banking go on a journey that goes beyond transactions and equips them with the knowledge and skills necessary to confidently and competently negotiate the complicated world of personal finance.

Digital Payment Methods

In the dynamic landscape of personal finance, the advent of digital payment methods has revolutionized the way individuals conduct transactions, offering a seamless and efficient alternative to traditional cash-based systems. This transformative shift extends beyond mere convenience, fundamentally altering the fabric of financial interactions and shaping the future of monetary transactions.

Central to the digital payment revolution is the prevalence of mobile wallets. These virtual repositories for funds have become integral to daily life, allowing users to effortlessly manage their money through smartphone applications. The simplicity of transferring funds, making purchases, and even splitting bills with friends has made mobile wallets a cornerstone of financial transactions, especially appealing to tech-savvy individuals seeking a streamlined and accessible approach to money management.

Contactless payment methods, utilizing Near Field Communication (NFC) technology, have also become ubiquitous. Enabling users to make secure transactions by simply tapping their cards or smartphones on compatible terminals, contactless payments minimize the reliance on physical currency. This not only expedites the checkout process but also aligns with a global push towards hygiene-conscious payment practices, particularly relevant in today's health-conscious environment.

Cryptocurrencies, a decentralized form of digital currency, represent a groundbreaking aspect of digital payments. While not yet mainstream, cryptocurrencies challenge traditional notions of money by operating outside centralized banking systems. The appeal lies in the potential for increased financial autonomy and borderless transactions. The ongoing evolution of this space prompts contemplation on the role of traditional currencies in a rapidly digitizing financial landscape.

Security is a paramount consideration in the widespread adoption of digital payment methods. Robust encryption, multi-factor authentication, and biometric verification measures are standard features implemented to safeguard users' financial information. The continuous refinement of security protocols reflects the commitment of the financial technology industry to instill confidence in users and overcome potential concerns regarding the safety of digital transactions.

Artificial intelligence (AI) and machine learning play a pivotal role in enhancing the user experience within digital payment systems. These technologies provide personalized insights, detect fraudulent activities, and offer predictive analytics. The ability of these systems to adapt and learn from user behavior not only ensures a more secure environment but also contributes to a tailored and efficient financial experience.

Beyond individual convenience, the widespread adoption of digital payments holds broader implications for the global economy. This shift prompts a reevaluation of regulatory frameworks and challenges traditional financial institutions to adapt to a changing landscape. Central banks and policymakers worldwide are faced with the task of navigating the implications of reduced reliance on physical currency and fostering an environment conducive to the continued growth of digital payment methods.

In essence, the rise of digital payment methods signifies more than a technological upgrade; it represents a fundamental restructuring of the way individuals interact with their finances. As we navigate this digital frontier, it is crucial to recognize the profound impact of these innovations on the financial ecosystem, shaping a future where accessibility, security, and efficiency converge to redefine the very essence of monetary transactions.

Understanding Online Security

Knowing internet security is essential to protecting your financial health in the connected world of digital banking. The need to safeguard your private data from potential dangers is increasing along with the popularity of digital interactions and online transactions. This understanding entails developing a proactive and knowledgeable approach to mitigate risks and guarantee a secure online financial experience; it goes beyond simply learning the fundamentals.

The term "online security" refers to a variety of procedures and safeguards intended to keep your money and personal data safe from fraud, illegal access, and online dangers. Here are important things to think about:

- **Strong Authentication Practices:** Embrace multi-factor authentication (MFA) whenever practicable. By demanding various kinds of authentication, such passwords, security codes, or biometrics, this provides an additional layer of safety.

- **Safe Password Management:** Give each of your internet accounts a strong, distinct password. Avoid using information that may be guessed, such as names or birthdays, and instead use a combination of letters, numbers, and symbols. To safely keep track of complicated passwords, think about utilizing trustworthy password management software.

- **Update Devices and Software Frequently:** Maintain the most recent versions of your operating system, antivirus program, and applications. Vulnerability fixes are frequently included in regular updates.

- **Watch Out for Phishing Attempts:** Exercise caution when responding to unsolicited calls, emails, or messages that request personal information. Reputable organizations won't use these methods to ask for private information. Before answering, confirm that the communication is genuine.

- **Employ Secure Networks:** Steer clear of using open Wi-Fi networks for sensitive transactions. Use password-protected, secure networks wherever possible, especially while accessing bank accounts or making online purchases.

- **Keep an eye on Account Activity:** Continually check your bank and credit card statements for any unusual or questionable transactions. Notify your banking institution of inconsistencies as soon as possible.

- **Encryption and Secure Websites:** Make sure that websites that deal with money have encrypted, secure connections. Examine the URL for "https://" and see if the address bar has a padlock icon.

- **Device Security:** Use biometric or password authentication to secure your gadgets. If your device becomes lost or stolen, turn on the tracking features.

- **Educate Yourself:** Remain aware of frequent internet frauds and threats. Knowing the strategies that fraudsters employ gives you the ability to identify and steer clear of such threats.

- **Frequent Data Backups:** Make frequent backups of your most crucial files and data. Having a backup assures you can recover important data in the case of a cyber disaster.

You strengthen your online security against potential cyber threats by adopting these measures. Online security requires constant vigilance and adaptation to changing threats; it is not a one-time decision. Recall that the preventive actions you do now help create a more secure and safe digital financial future.

CHAPTER 5: INVESTING FOR TEENS

Introduction to Investment

For many youngsters, the idea of investing is foreign ground when it comes to personal finance. But the first step in creating a safe financial future is knowing the fundamentals of investing. We'll dive into the realm of investing for teenagers in this chapter, covering both the mentality and the practical aspects that can lead to long-term financial success.

Investing is simply working with your money in the hopes of making a profit. Teenagers typically start with understanding compound interest, which is the notion that money can grow astronomically over time. Imagine sowing a seed that becomes a sturdy tree with time and care. Comparably, investing means sowing financial seeds that, if they flourish, will yield a bountiful harvest later on.

The stock market is a vital tool for adolescent investors. A stock purchase makes you a shareholder in the company, and stocks symbolize ownership in it. But the stock market may be erratic, so it's critical to comprehend the advantages and disadvantages. By investigating low-risk options like index funds or exchange-traded funds (ETFs), teens can dabble in investing. By distributing risk among several businesses, these diversified investments provide a more reliable entry point into the market.

Furthermore, investment is a wider field than just equities. Bonds are simply loans given to governments or enterprises in exchange for regular interest payments; teens can investigate these. Although they could yield lesser returns than stocks, bonds are typically thought to carry less risk.

Real estate is yet another option to think about. Even if buying a home could be a long-term goal, a teen's view on money might be expanded by learning about real estate as an investment. Investing in real estate without holding actual property is possible with real estate investment trusts (REITs).

It's important to introduce risk tolerance to kids as they navigate the world of investment. All investments involve some level of risk, and building a diverse portfolio starts with knowing how comfortable you are with risk. When it comes to investing, the proverb "don't put all your eggs in one basket" is especially applicable.

Beyond the specifics, developing a long-term perspective is essential. Investing is a marathon, not a sprint, and it's not a get-rich-quick program. It is important to teach teenagers that financial objectives should be reasonable and that investment values are subject to change. A necessary component of the investing process is making calculated decisions and exercising patience during these ups and downs.

Teens can also learn about investing responsibly, which helps them match their financial decisions to their moral principles. This entails evaluating businesses' governance, social, and environmental aspects (ESG) prior to making an investment in them. Young investors can earn money and support issues they care about at the same time.

Finally, it's critical to comprehend the impact of consistent contributions. Compounding allows even modest, steady investments to grow substantially over time. It can significantly impact a teen's financial future to encourage early investment and sustained commitment to a long-term plan.

In conclusion, developing a financial stewardship mindset is more important for young investors than simply looking at data and market patterns. It's a path requiring patience, risk evaluation, and education. Teens can create a solid foundation for a financially secure future in which they manage their money wisely and expand it exponentially as they venture down the fascinating path of personal finance by learning the fundamentals of investing and embracing a long-term outlook.

Exploring Investment Options

Examining investment possibilities gives them access to a vibrant and varied world that extends beyond conventional savings options. This section will elucidate the diverse pathways that are accessible, each possessing distinct attributes and opportunities for advancement.

- **Stocks**: Purchasing individual stocks entitles the investor to a portion of the company. With this option, teenagers can become shareholders and possibly earn dividends and capital appreciation from the company's performance. Although it is a vibrant and interesting field, stock market volatility is a given.

- **Bonds**: Generally regarded as a more cautious option, bonds entail lending money to governments or businesses in return for regular interest payments and the principal amount returned when the bond matures. Bonds have a more consistent return than stocks, despite typically carrying less risk.

- **Mutual funds:** These investment vehicles combine the capital of several individuals to purchase a variety of stocks, bonds, and other assets. This alternative provides diversity without making teenagers choose specific stocks. On behalf of the investors, qualified fund managers make investment decisions.

- **Exchange-Traded Funds (ETFs):** ETFs are collections of assets that resemble indexes, much like mutual funds. The main distinction is that ETFs, like actual stocks, are traded on stock exchanges. Compared to certain mutual funds, they have cheaper costs and offer liquidity and diversification.

- **Real Estate Investment Trusts (REITs):** REITs provide an affordable option for individuals who are interested in real estate but aren't quite ready to purchase a home. Investors in these trusts earn dividends based on the rental revenue and capital gains from the sales of income-producing real estate.

- **Cryptocurrencies:** Although they are still relatively new to the financial world, alternative investments like Bitcoin and Ethereum are gaining traction. Teenagers should exercise caution and have a solid grasp of the market while considering this choice, though, as they carry a significant level of risk and volatility.

- **Certificates of Deposit (CDs) and savings accounts:** are safe places to save money, even if they aren't classic investments in the sense that they yield big returns. They offer liquidity and are perfect for emergency funds or short-term objectives.

- **Education Savings Accounts (ESAs):** With tax benefits, ESAs are specifically created for educational expenses. Both contributions and withdrawals for approved educational costs are tax-free. Contributions increase tax-free.

It is important to highlight the concept of risk and reward when youth investigate various possibilities. Every investing path has a unique set of hazards, thus building a well-balanced portfolio requires knowing one's risk tolerance. Investing across a variety of asset types, or diversification, can reduce risk and maximize rewards.

Participating in continuing financial education is also essential. Markets change, therefore it's important for teens to stay up to date on economic trends, investment techniques, and the state of the world economy in order to make wise judgments.

Through the process of investigating investment choices, teenagers not only acquire financial literacy but also develop critical thinking, decision-making, and long-term planning skills, all vital building blocks for a financially astute future.

The Power of Compound Interest

For young people who have the luxury of time on their side, the power of compound interest is a financial phenomena that has the potential to completely transform the investing landscape. Fundamentally, compound interest is the idea of earning interest on the principal amount as well as the interest that has accrued over time from prior periods. Put more simply, it's the idea of interest earning interest, which has the potential to greatly increase an investment's growth over time.

Teens must first realize the value of starting early in order to fully utilize compound interest. One important component of this equation is time. An investment has more time to compound and expand the earlier it is made. This is known as the "time value of money," and it's a concept that, in the long run, can make even little contributions grow into substantial sums.

Let's examine the operation of compound interest:

- **Initial Principal:** The original principal is the sum of money you deposit or invest. This is the starting point for any financial activities, such as funding a retirement account, investing in stocks, or saving money.

- **Interest Earnings:** The original principal accrues interest over time. Compound interest is special because, in contrast to simple interest, it applies to both the initial amount and the interest that has accrued over time.

- **Accumulation Over Time:** The investment increases with each compounding period—monthly, quarterly, or annual—due to the compounding effect on the interest earned as well as the initial contribution. As a result, there is a snowball effect and the investment grows more quickly.

Consider investing $1,000, for instance, with a 5% annual interest rate that is compounded every year. You would receive $50 in interest after the first year, for a total of $1,050. You would get interest on the $1,000 that you started with as well as the $50 that you earned the first year in the second year. This compounding process keeps exponential growth going throughout time.

When investing for a long time, compound interest becomes especially important. With time on their side, teens can see many times returns on their investments. This emphasizes how crucial it is to make constant contributions and how important patience is when investing.

In order to fully utilize compound interest, teenagers should concentrate on:

- **Regular Contributions**: Increasing the compounding benefit of an investment requires regular contributions, no matter how small.

- **Reinvesting Earnings**: By reinvesting interest earnings, you may maximize the compounding effect and lessen the need to cash out your earnings.

- **Long-Term View:** Having an understanding of compound interest's progressive nature serves to highlight the significance of adopting a long-term investing perspective.

In summary, compound interest is an ally in finance that gets stronger with time. Understanding and utilizing this power might be crucial for young people just starting out in the world of investing to create a solid and stable financial future.

CHAPTER 6: CREDIT AND DEBT

Demystifying Credit Scores

For teenagers venturing into the realm of personal finance, deciphering credit ratings is an essential first step. Lenders use credit scores, which are numerical representations of a person's creditworthiness, to determine how risky it is to lend money or provide credit. To behave responsibly with money, one must comprehend credit scores, their components, importance, and management.

What Makes Up a Credit Score:

- Payment History (35%): The payment history accounts for the largest portion of a credit score. Paying bills, credit accounts, and loans on time has a favorable impact on credit score; late payments, defaults, and bankruptcies have a negative one.

- Credit Utilization (30%): This percentage assesses how much credit has been used relative to its overall availability. Maintaining low credit card balances in comparison to credit limits raises credit score.

- Length of Credit History (15%): The amount of time a credit account has been open is important. A longer credit history can improve a credit score by demonstrating a history of careful credit management.

- Credit Account Types in Use (10%): Lenders value variety in the credit accounts that a person oversees, including retail, installment loans, and credit cards.

- New Credit (10%): Opening many credit accounts quickly may be seen as risky. It is advisable to handle and distribute new credit applications.

Relevance of Credit Ratings:

- Loan Approval and Interest Rates: Having a better credit score makes it more likely that a loan will be approved and may also result in lower interest rates. This holds true for a variety of loans, such as personal, auto, and home loans.

- Credit Card Approval and Limitations: When accepting applications and setting credit limits, credit card issuers frequently take credit scores into account. Having a high credit score can help you get better card deals.

- Employment Opportunities: Credit ratings may be examined by certain companies during the employment process, particularly for roles with financial responsibility.

- Renting a Home: During the rental application process, landlords may run credit checks. Getting a better score can increase your chances of getting a lease.

Controlling and Enhancing Credit Ratings:

- On-Time Payments: It's critical to always make payments on schedule. To guarantee on-time arrival, set up automated payments or reminders.

- Credit Utilization: Maintain a modest credit card balance in comparison to your credit limit. Try to keep your utilization rate under 30%.

- Diversify Your Credit Accounts: A variety of credit kinds, including installment loans and credit cards, might raise your credit score.

- Check Credit Reports Frequently: Keep an eye out for mistakes and illegal activity on credit reports. Every one of the main credit bureaus offers free annual credit reports.

- Avoid Opening Needless Credit Accounts: Creating impulsive new account openings can have a bad effect on credit score, even though having a choice of credit kinds is advantageous.

Teens who understand credit scores are better equipped to handle money properly. Teens can set themselves up for future financial stability and a strong credit foundation by learning the elements that affect credit scores and forming excellent credit history-building behaviors.

Responsible Use of Credit

A key component of financial literacy for teenagers is responsible credit utilization, which paves the way for a sound and long-lasting financial future. When utilized sensibly, credit may be an effective instrument for managing financial demands and attaining objectives. Here is a manual for comprehending and using credit responsibly:

Understanding Credit

- **What is Credit?** In essence, credit is borrowed funds that you can use to pay bills or buy purchases. It gives you access to money on the condition that you return the borrowed sum, frequently with interest.

- **Types of credit:** There are various forms of credit, including credit cards, personal loans, student loans, and mortgages. Each type serves different purposes, such as short-term spending flexibility or long-term investments like home ownership.

Guidelines for Conscientious Use of Credit

- **Only Borrow What You Can Repay**: Consider your repayment capacity before utilizing credit. Make sure you borrow no more than you can afford to repay within the specified time frame.

- **Recognize Interest Rates:** Credit has expenses associated with it, typically in the form of interest. Recognize how the interest rates on your credit accounts affect the total amount you have to pay back.

- **Make and Follow a Budget**: Having a budget enables you to handle your money more skillfully. Understand your earnings, outgoings, and the maximum amount you can set aside for debt repayment without jeopardizing your ability to make ends meet.

- **Pay on Time:** Maintaining a good credit history requires timely payments. In addition to costing you money, late payments can lower your credit score.

- **Keep an Eye on Your Credit Score:** Verify the correctness of your credit score and reports on a regular basis to spot any possible problems. Knowing your credit score makes it easier for you to determine your creditworthiness.

- **Avoid Maxing Out Credit Limits**: Your credit score may suffer if you have large credit card balances in comparison to your credit limit. Try to maintain credit card balances under 30% of available credit.

- **Think Long-Term:** Take into account how your credit decisions will affect you down the road. Using credit responsibly now might lead to better terms on loans down the road, like a mortgage or auto loan.

Establishing Credit Wisely

- **Start Small:** To build a credit history if you don't already have any, think about applying for a secured credit card or adding yourself as an authorized user on a family member's credit card.

- **Diversify Your Credit Types:** Having a variety of credit kinds, including installment loans and credit cards, might raise your credit score. But refrain from creating pointless accounts.

- **Show Consistency:** A stable credit history is valued by lenders. Demonstrate your ability to manage credit responsibly over time by keeping your credit card balances low and paying your bills on time.

- **Proactively Handle Financial Difficulties:** As soon as you run into financial difficulties, get in touch with your creditors. If you're proactive in looking for answers, a lot of creditors are prepared to cooperate with you.

Responsible credit utilization is essentially about making thoughtful, purposeful decisions that support your financial objectives. It's a tool that can support stability and prosperity in terms of money if used properly. Teenagers may confidently traverse the credit environment and lay a solid basis for their financial future by grasping the fundamentals of appropriate credit use.

Understanding Debt

Gaining a knowledge of the dynamics of debt is a critical first step toward achieving financial literacy in the maze of personal finance. Debt is sometimes seen as a two-edged sword: while it can open doors and fulfill aspirations, it can also be abused to cause financial instability. Understanding the intricacies of debt is essential for teenagers navigating the financial world since it will enable them to make wise and responsible financial decisions.

Debt is essentially a responsibility to repay money that has been borrowed. It takes many different forms, each with unique ramifications and effects on one's financial security. Credit cards, personal loans, mortgages, and student loans are a few prevalent types of debt that people deal with at different points in their lives.

Student loans are the initial source of debt for a lot of people. Even if a person's education is an investment in their future, student loan debt can have a lasting impact. It is essential to comprehend the conditions of these loans, including interest rates and payback schedules. It's not only about the amount borrowed; it's also about the money's overall cost.

Credit cards offer a practical way to make purchases and are frequently associated with achieving financial freedom. They do, however, also offer a temptation to overspend. The simplicity of using a card to make a transaction can sometimes mask the fact that each one is actually a tiny loan. Interest is charged on unpaid credit card debt, and even the minimum payment merely scratches the surface. This can result in a vicious cycle of debt that is difficult to break free from.

In contrast, mortgages are a significant and frequently required obligation for people who want to become homeowners. Mortgages come with the obligation of making consistent payments, even though they let people and families fulfill their ambition of owning a home. Comprehending the conditions of a mortgage, such as interest rates, loan duration, and the influence of down payments, enables people to make knowledgeable choices regarding homeownership.

Knowing the idea of interest is crucial, even beyond the different kinds of debt. The cost of borrowing money is called interest, and it is calculated as a percentage of the total amount borrowed. The interest rate has a big impact on the total amount paid back over time, whether it's a credit card or a loan. Determining the true cost of borrowed money requires an understanding of how interest rates affect debt.

Debt management calls for a careful balance. On the one side, carefully managing debt can help you reach your financial objectives, like making an investment in your schooling, buying a house, or launching a business. Conversely, high or poorly managed debt can cause financial strain and hinder one's capacity to meet long-term goals.

Most importantly, having debt is not always a bad thing. For many people and homes, it is a financial reality. How one handles and navigates that debt is what counts. Comprehending loan terms, paying back loans on time, and keeping an eye on one's overall financial situation are all necessary components of responsible borrowing.

CHAPTER 7: TAXES FOR TEENS

Two essential components of financial literacy are paying taxes correctly and managing one's finances. This part will give you a general introduction of taxes, walk you through the teenage tax filing procedure, and stress the value of sound financial management.

Understanding Taxes

Teenagers' perception of civic duty and the operation of society is greatly influenced by their understanding of taxes. Taxes are mandatory financial contributions levied by the government on people and organizations in order to finance infrastructure and public services. Teens need to understand that paying taxes is about more than just saving money; it's about making a positive impact on the community.

There are many different types of taxes, such as sales tax, property tax, income tax, and more. Taxes on income are imposed on the money that people get from working, investing, or working for themselves. Teens who comprehend this tax are better able to appreciate the worth of their income and how some of it goes toward funding public services like infrastructure, healthcare, and education.

When goods and services are purchased, sales tax is paid. Teenagers can better understand how sales tax affects their spending patterns and how much money it brings in for local and state governments by learning about it. Property taxes, which are levied on property owners, provide information about how public spaces like parks and schools are maintained.

Teenagers who understand the rationale behind taxes are also better able to appreciate the social compact, which outlines how citizens fund the government in return for public services. It emphasizes the value of being involved in the democratic process, where people can influence how tax dollars are spent by electing representatives, and it cultivates a sense of civic duty.

Adolescents who comprehend taxes are more capable of making wise financial choices.

Understanding tax credits, deductions, and brackets can help with long-term budgeting. They can learn how to handle their money, file tax returns, and understand how taxes affect their life and goals for the future.

Furthermore, knowing taxes encourages critical analysis of societal problems. It promotes discussions about the equity and fairness of the tax system by encouraging people to question the methods used to collect and distribute taxes. Teens who possess this knowledge are more equipped to discuss economic policies and how they affect society in conversations.

Types of Taxes

There are numerous extremely prevalent tax types:

1. Income tax: is the portion of earned income that is given to the federal or state governments.
2. Payroll tax: is a portion of an employee's income that is deducted by their employer and sent to the government on their behalf to support Social Security and Medicare.

3. Corporate tax: is the portion of a company's profits that the government withholds in order to pay for federal programs.
4. Sales tax: Depending on the jurisdiction, taxes are imposed on specific goods and services.
5. Property tax: based on the value of land and property assets.
6. Tariffs: are levied on imports with the intention of bolstering home companies.
7. The estate tax: is a rate that is applied on the fair market value (FMV) of the assets in a deceased person's estate; the entire estate must be more than the limits established by the federal and state governments.

Navigating Tax Forms

Even though navigating tax forms may appear difficult, with a little help, you can understand the intricacies and carry out your civic duty. Understanding the forms involved in taxes ensures a more seamless procedure and may even result in financial benefits. Tax season is an annual ritual.

Many forms, each with a distinct function, are at the center of the tax filing process. Individuals most frequently use the 1040 series, which consists of the 1040, 1040A, and 1040EZ. The form you select will rely on your financial circumstances. The most comprehensive form, 1040, is appropriate for people with a variety of income streams and deductions. Simpler versions, the 1040A and 1040EZ, are intended for people with less complicated financial profiles.

An important document that summarizes your income and the taxes deducted by your employer for the entire year is the W-2 form. It is important to confirm the correctness of the information on your W-2 because inaccuracies may have an impact on your tax liability.

The 1099 papers are relevant if you received money from self-employment or freelance jobs. There are other kinds of 1099 forms, including 1099-INT for interest income and 1099-NEC for non-employee compensation. These documents, which list extra income from sources other than regular work, need to be included on your tax return.

One of the main ways to lower taxable income is through deductions, which you itemize on the Schedule A form. Medical costs, charitable contributions, and mortgage interest are examples of common deductions. It's crucial to know which costs can be written off in order to optimize your tax advantages.

Tax credits linked to education can help with the cost of tuition. You can claim credits like the American Opportunity Credit and the Lifetime Learning Credit with the use of the 1098-T form, which offers information on educational expenses.

The 1099-R form describes dividends for those who made contributions to retirement funds, like an IRA or 401(k). To determine the amount of taxes due on withdrawals from these accounts, this information is essential.

The IRS provides a number of online tools and services to help with the tax filing process, which can be completed on paper or electronically. Make sure the software or provider you've chosen supports the forms that apply to your situation when filing electronically.

Maintaining structured records all year long is crucial to reducing the stress of tax season. Keep a file with all of your receipts, income records, and other pertinent documents. This procedure helps to expedite the filing process and provides a useful record for future financial planning or audits.

Your Responsibilities as a Taxpayer

You bear a set of obligations as a taxpayer that are essential to a well-functioning society. Comprehending and carrying out these responsibilities not only guarantees adherence to tax regulations but also enhances the community's overall welfare. The following are the principal duties associated with being a taxpayer:

- Precise Income Reporting: It is your duty to provide correct information about all of your sources of income. This covers all types of earnings, such as dividends, self-employment income, and wages.

- Paying Taxes on Time: It's important to remember when to file your taxes. In order to avoid fines and interest, it is imperative that you file your tax return by the designated deadline, which in the US is often April 15.

- Choosing the Correct Tax Form: It's important to make sure the tax form you choose fits your financial circumstances. Using the appropriate form, whether it's the 1040, 1040A, or 1040EZ, guarantees accurate reporting.

- Keeping Records: Ensure that you have well-organized records of your earnings, outlays, and pertinent paperwork. This procedure not only makes tax filing easier, but it also acts as a guide for audits and other questions.

- Recognizing Deductions and Credits: To lawfully reduce your tax liability, familiarize yourself with the deductions and credits that apply to you. This covers deductions for various tax credits that can be applicable to you, homeownership, and educational costs.

- Fulfilling Tax Liabilities: It is your duty to settle any outstanding taxes by the due date. Penalties and interest costs may arise from failing to pay taxes on time or ignoring them.

- Reacting to Correspondence: Pay close attention to any correspondence you get from tax officials. To prevent issues, reply to questions, notifications, or requests for more information right away.

- Maintaining Up-to-Date Information: Notify the tax authorities of any changes to your address, marital status, or other noteworthy events in your life that might have an impact on your tax situation.

- Getting Professional counsel When Necessary: You should think about getting counsel from tax professionals if you have questions regarding tax regulations or if your financial position is complicated. Their knowledge can guide you through complex tax situations.

- Contributing to Retirement funds: Make use of retirement funds that offer tax advantages. In addition to securing your financial future, making contributions to these accounts might have tax advantages.

- Recognizing Tax Law Changes: Keep yourself updated on any modifications to the tax code. Deductions, credits, and other tax-related factors may change due to legislation; staying up to date on these developments guarantees that you are making wise financial decisions.

- Engaging in Civic Responsibilities: Acknowledge that taxes support infrastructure and public services. Making your fair share of contributions guarantees the operation of all government programs, including defense and education.

CHAPTER 8: ENTREPRENEURSHIP FOR TEENS

Starting a business as a teenager may be a thrilling and life-changing event. Beyond the conventional notions of employment, entrepreneurship provides a platform for personal development, creativity, and invention.

Unleashing Your Entrepreneurial Spirit

When it comes to teenage dreams, the concept of entrepreneurship frequently inspires feelings of possibility and excitement. It might be exciting and intimidating to consider converting your passion into a business and making something entirely original. "Unleashing Your Entrepreneurial Spirit" is about adopting a mindset that encourages creativity, resilience, and an original approach to problem-solving, rather than just launching a firm.

Fundamentally, entrepreneurship is a process of self-discovery. It involves determining your aptitudes, interests, and the issues you are deeply committed to resolving. You may be wondering, "Can I really be an entrepreneur at this age?" as a teenager. Without a doubt, the answer is yes. The spirit of entrepreneurship has no age restrictions, as seen by the numerous success tales of young, successful business owners throughout history.

So where do you even start? Begin with a strong desire. What lights a fire under your soul? Which issues do you feel driven to address, whether they are local or global in nature? Finding these passions will be the first step in your entrepreneurial path. Perhaps you have an interest in fashion, technology, or environmental issues. Your passion, whatever it may be, is what will keep you going as an entrepreneur.

Developing your enthusiasm into a well-thought-out concept is the next stage. What can you produce or offer that meets a demand or resolves an issue? This could be a service, a good, or even a charitable endeavor. Think about the tale of a teenage girl who founded a neighborhood recycling program because she was so concerned about environmental sustainability. This project not only benefited the neighborhood but also sparked a feeling of achievement and purpose.

Being an entrepreneur is considerably more than just having big ideas—it's about starting something. This could entail creating a prototype, speaking with prospective clients, or carrying out market research. It involves making your idea a genuine, attainable reality. Recall that being an entrepreneur is frequently an iterative process. Your original concept may change as you get input and gain experience.

Entrepreneurs that are successful are known for their resilience. There will be difficulties, and failures are unavoidable. But these are the times when your entrepreneurial spirit is really put to the test. Accept setbacks as teaching moments and see roadblocks as opportunities to improve. What distinguishes entrepreneurs is their capacity for change, adaptation, and persistence.

Another important component of entrepreneurship is teamwork. Look for mentors, counselors, or like-minded people who can offer direction and encouragement. Taking in knowledge from the experiences of others can help you grow faster. Think about attending workshops, networking with experts in your field of interest, and joining regional or virtual entrepreneurial communities.

As you set out on your entrepreneurial path, keep in mind that success isn't exclusively determined by profit. It's about influence, personal development, and the fulfillment that comes from pursuing a worthwhile goal. Entrepreneurship imparts important life skills that go well beyond the economic world, such as resilience, problem-solving, and communication.

Turning Hobbies into Income

Imagine being able to combine your passion and practicality by making what you love become more than simply a hobby or a way to make money. "Turning Hobbies into Income" is a voyage of discovery that looks at how you may use your skills and interests to become financially empowered in addition to being a source of personal fulfillment.

Passionate pursuits of hobbies are often the foundation of prosperous businesses. The first step in any endeavor is to appreciate your passion, whether it be writing, gaming, creating, or anything else. Your pastime has the potential to develop into a distinctive and marketable ability, so it's not just a way to kill time.

Finding a market for your activity is essential. Who else is passionate like you, and how can you satisfy their needs or wants? If you're a passionate painter, for instance, you might want to sell your pieces or provide painting lessons. If you're really good at a certain video game, look into opportunities in content development or gaming tournaments.

Using digital platforms is often necessary to turn a passion into a source of revenue. People now have never-before-seen opportunities to market and promote their talents because of the internet. Establish a presence online via social media, a personal website, or specialized venues for your pastime. This gives you a platform to interact with possible clients or customers in addition to broadening your reach.

Depending on your objectives and hobby, there are several monetization options to choose from. It can be profitable to sell goods like prints, digital downloads, or merchandise for creative endeavors like writing, painting, or music. If your pastime requires a certain skill set, you could want to consider providing services, guides, or customized experiences.

When converting interests into a source of revenue, consistency and quality are essential. Maintain a standard of quality that makes you stand out as you shift from enjoying yourself personally to thinking like a businessperson. This could entail investing in better equipment, honing your craft, or persistently looking for new and creative methods to operate within your specialty.

Collaboration and networking are effective instruments for this trip. Make connections with like-minded individuals in your hobby community and associated fields. Partnerships may increase your reach, present you with fresh prospects, and give you insightful knowledge about the industry.

It's critical to control expectations and strike a balance in order to keep your pastime enjoyable. Long-term success depends on retaining the inner desire that drew you to the pastime in the first place, even though turning it into a source of money can be satisfying.

Building a Simple Business Plan

Any company effort, no matter how little, needs to have a roadmap, a set of instructions that describes your objectives, tactics, and course of action. "Building a Simple Business Plan" is the tool you need to turn your creative ideas into a well-organized game plan.

- Executive Summary: Give a succinct rundown of your company's operations first. Describe the problem or need your product or service solves, your mission, and your business idea.

- Examine your company's essence in greater detail in your business description. Which goods and services are you going to provide? What makes your company unique, and who is your target market?

- Conduct market research on rivals, market trends, and your industry. Determine your target audience and demonstrate your grasp of their requirements and preferences.

- Structure and Administration: Describe the organization of your company. What positions do the important team members hold and who are they? Emphasize your experience and abilities that are pertinent.

- Line of Products or Services: Give thorough details about the services you are providing. What qualities and advantages are there? What needs does it address for your intended audience?

- Sales and Marketing: Describe your sales and marketing plans in detail. How are you going to market your company? Which platforms will you employ to connect with your intended audience? Add in the selling strategies and price.

- Funds Request (if applicable): Please provide information about the amount, the intended use, and the anticipated results of any funds that you are requesting. Having this component is essential to luring lenders or investors.

- Financial Projections: Provide accurate and reasonable financial estimates. Add anticipated cash flow, balance sheet, and income statement projections. This part shows that you are aware of the financial aspects of your company.

- Appendix: Provide any further details you feel are necessary, such as market research data, key team member resumes, or other pertinent documents.

Creating a basic business plan is more than just a formality; it's a strategic process that makes you define your goals and engage in critical thinking about your company. It functions as a communication tool when looking for partnerships or support, a reference point for goals, and a tool for decision-making.

Recall that simplicity is essential. Stakeholders are more likely to comprehend and approve of a business strategy that is succinct and straightforward. It is a dynamic document that will alter and grow with your company. Maintaining your focus on your goal can help you write a business plan where each section works toward the success of your venture as a whole.

CHAPTER 9: CULTIVATING A SAVINGS MINDSET

A savings attitude is a thread in the personal finance tapestry that leads to financial freedom and resilience. It takes more than just practice to develop this mindset; it's a life-changing experience that affects how you handle uncertainty in life as well as how you relate to money.

Fundamentally, a savings mindset is based on the understanding that money is a tool for building the future you want, not just a medium of exchange. It's about accepting the notion that saving a percentage of your income is a conscious and powerful decision rather than a drudgery. Let's explore the fundamentals of developing a savings attitude and the reasons it's essential to sound financial management.

Modifying Viewpoints

The first step in developing a savings attitude is perspective. It's important to see saving as a way to give yourself financial security and independence rather than as a way to cut down on your spending. Consider it an investment in your future self rather than a sacrifice. This change creates the groundwork for a more positive relationship with money, one that values stability above short-term satisfaction.

Accepting Postponed Gratification

Developing a savings mindset is a discipline in accepting delayed satisfaction in a society that frequently promotes rapid gratification. It entails stifling the need to blow every dollar as soon as it comes into your pocket and realizing the value of gradually building up funds for objectives down the road. This ability develops resilience in the face of unforeseen difficulties in addition to financial discipline.

Creating Intentional Goals

A savings mindset gathers steam when it is rooted in worthwhile objectives. Having a specific goal offers your savings direction and purpose, whether it's for a business endeavor, a dream vacation, or education. As guiding lights, goals help you make financial decisions and strengthen the link between what you do now and what you want to achieve in the future.

Honoring Financial Achievements

Developing a savings attitude involves appreciating and enjoying the road as much as the outcome. Any accomplishment, no matter how little, demonstrates your discipline and dedication. Every accomplishment, whether it's hitting a savings goal or overcoming the need to make an impulsive buy, serves to strengthen the good behaviors that form the foundation of a savings mindset.

Handling Difficulties

There are obstacles in the way of adopting a savings attitude. Your dedication may be put to the test by unforeseen costs, peer pressure, and the seduction of instant gratification. But it's crucial to see these difficulties as chances for development rather than as failures. A crucial component of developing a savings mindset is building resilience, which will allow you to adjust and continue on your path when faced with financial difficulties.

Creating a Long-Term Routine

Cultivating a savings attitude involves practice and consistency, just like any other habit. As your financial condition improves, gradually raise your contributions, start small, and automate your saves if you can. The idea is to turn saving from a conscious effort into a subliminal habit by integrating it organically into your financial routine.

The Ability to Transform

To put it simply, developing a savings attitude is a life-changing experience that goes beyond money. It imparts self-control, endurance, and a feeling of direction that permeates all facets of your life. The abilities developed on this journey resilience, goal-setting, and financial discipline become invaluable tools for overcoming the challenges of daily life.

As you set out on your life-changing adventure, keep in mind that developing a savings mindset is a continuous effort rather than a one-time accomplishment. It's about developing a healthy, long-lasting relationship with money that gives you the ability to confidently and purposefully traverse life's financial terrain. By adopting this mentality, you not only safeguard your financial future but also pave the way for a life that is characterized by options rather than limitations.

The Psychology of Saving

More than merely putting money away, developing a savings attitude is a psychological journey that molds your connection with money and paves the road for a stable financial future. We'll examine the several factors that affect how we save money in this investigation of the psychology of saving, as well as how comprehending these dynamics can help kids make better financial decisions.

Fundamentally, saving is an action based on self-control and foresight. It entails choosing long-term security over the temptation of instant satisfaction. The capacity to forgo a smaller reward now in favor of a larger reward later on is known as delayed gratification, and it is one of the core psychological concepts at work. Gaining proficiency in this area is like exercising a mental muscle: the more you use it, the stronger it gets.

Goal-setting and the idea of delayed gratification are related. You give your financial decisions a purpose when you establish precise savings goals. Having a specific goal gives you motivation to save money for things like an emergency fund, a dream vacation, or even a gadget. Savings becomes a meaningful undertaking with the help of this psychological anchor, which makes it easier to resist impulsive purchasing.

Social impact is yet another potent factor influencing how we save. Our attitudes on money are greatly influenced by family, society expectations, and peer pressure. Teens can negotiate the fine line between gratifying their current social needs and laying a solid financial foundation by being aware of these factors. The goal is to strike a balance between making ethical financial decisions and being involved in society.

Furthermore, saving can often be significantly hampered psychologically by a dread of the unknown. Teens may struggle with future uncertainty, which makes them reluctant to save money. Developing a financial resilience mindset—the conviction that having savings offers a safety net and a sense of control—is essential to overcoming this worry. This mental change is essential to changing saving from a cause of worry to an empowerment tool.

Behavioral economists frequently draw attention to the significance of mental accounting, a theory that describes how people divide their money in their minds. Teens' attitude to saving money could be completely changed by understanding this issue. Teenagers who approach money holistically rather than arbitrarily classifying it into several groups are better equipped to make financial decisions. This mental accounting integration makes the savings plan more efficient and well-rounded.

Furthermore, it is impossible to overlook the impact of cognitive biases in the psychology of saving. For example, kids may seek information that supports their already attitudes about money due to confirmation bias. A more unbiased and knowledgeable approach to saving is made possible by acknowledging and combating these prejudices.

The psychological impact of saving is heavily influenced by the emotional bond with money. Building a positive relationship with finances requires a knowledge of the frequently observed relationship between money and emotions. Emotional spending motivated by happiness, anxiety, or boredom can ruin even the best-laid plans for savings. Gaining financial emotional intelligence enables teenagers to make deliberate purchasing decisions that are consistent with their morals.

To sum up, the psychology of saving is a complex field that combines social dynamics, behavioral economics, and emotional intelligence. Teens who understand these nuances can turn saving from a difficult chore into a fulfilling and self-empowering habit. It's important to comprehend the psychological dynamics at work in order to create a robust and meaningful financial future. It's not just about the numbers.

Overcoming Common Saving Challenges

Although it's a noble objective, saving money might present some difficulties. It takes a combination of discipline, planning, and a clear awareness of the typical roadblocks that people, even teenagers, may experience to overcome these difficulties. Let's examine some of these difficulties and methods for overcoming them.

- Absence of Budgeting. Not knowing where your money is going is one of the biggest obstacles to saving. Making a budget is the remedy for this problem. Teens can take charge of their financial situation and find areas where they can make savings by keeping track of their income and expenses.

- Impulse Spending: In a world full of alluring trends and commercials, the temptation of making impulsive purchases can be very powerful. Spending with awareness is necessary to overcome this obstacle. Consider whether a purchase will fit into your financial goals before making it. Setting a waiting time for purchases of non-essential items can aid in reducing impulsive behavior.

- Peer Pressure: Social interactions have a big impact on how people spend their money. Adolescents frequently experience peer pressure to emulate their classmates' spending habits. Finding a balance between financial responsibility and social participation is necessary to overcome this obstacle. Open communication about financial objectives among friends can foster a community that supports frugal spending.

- Fixed Allowance: A lot of teenagers get a certain amount of money each month, which might not always be enough to cover their expenses or save money. To get past this obstacle, look into other revenue streams. A greater degree of financial management flexibility can be obtained by diversifying revenue streams, whether through part-time employment, freelance work, or the use of creative abilities.

- Emergency Expenses: Even the best-laid plans can be derailed by unforeseen financial difficulties. One of the most important aspects of financial resilience is creating an emergency fund. Teens can be ready for unforeseen financial setbacks without letting their long-term savings goals slip by designating a specified portion of their pay for such purposes.

- Low Income: Teens may struggle with having little money, especially if they don't have any part-time work. To get around this, concentrate on making the most savings with the resources at hand. This could entail haggling over funds with guardians or parents, looking into ways to reduce expenses, and coming up with inventive ways to increase income, such as taking on side jobs or starting a business.

- Absence of Financial Education: Not having access to financial education is a big problem for a lot of teenagers. A dedication to self-learning is necessary to get past this obstacle. To improve financial literacy, make use of resources like books, online courses, and trustworthy financial websites. Seek advice from mentors or family members who are knowledgeable about finances as well.

- Short-Term Thinking: Savings efforts may be hampered by the tendency to put short-term necessities ahead of long-term wants. Create a future-focused vision in order to overcome this obstacle. Establish attainable financial objectives that will inspire you and give you a feeling of direction. Reaching significant milestones might provide a greater sense of satisfaction than instant fulfillment when one adopts an optimistic outlook.

Celebrating Financial Milestones

Celebrating financial accomplishments is an important but sometimes disregarded part of the personal finance journey. Your financial mentality and general well-being can be greatly impacted by pausing to recognize and celebrate your accomplishments as you navigate the world of budgeting, saving, investing, and making wise financial decisions.

Financial milestones include all of the little victories and stages that are accomplished along the route, not only the attainment of a set goal or a certain monetary sum. Imagine contributing to your savings regularly, keeping to your budget for multiple consecutive months, or making your first investment all achievements deserving of celebration.

Celebrating financial achievements is important since it encourages positive behavior. Recognizing and appreciating your accomplishments helps you maintain the routines and behaviors that lead to your financial success. This encouraging feedback starts a motivational cycle that increases the likelihood that you'll keep making wise financial decisions.

Marking financial achievements with celebration also offers a chance for introspection. Consider where you were a moment ago and acknowledge the progress you have made. By thinking back on your financial path, you can better understand your habits, assets, and places for development. It enables you to hone your future objectives and plans of action, forging a more deliberate route to financial security.

Additionally, acknowledging financial achievements fosters thankfulness. Acknowledging your successes, no matter how minor, fosters gratitude for the tools and chances that helped you succeed. This thankfulness goes beyond material possessions; it cultivates an optimistic and appreciative attitude that can enhance other facets of your life.

Financial achievements also act as a reminder of your strength and fortitude. Overcoming obstacles is a necessary component of the process towards achieving financial well-being, which is not always an easy path. By commemorating accomplishments, you show that you can grow, change with the times, and keep going, which gives you more confidence to face financial obstacles in the future.

Finally, the goal of commemorating financial achievements is to relish the trip. Personal finance is about the ongoing development, learning, and evolution of your financial life rather than just reaching a destination. In the long run, the journey becomes more sustainable and enjoyable when you take the time to celebrate your accomplishments since it brings joy to the process.

In summary, acknowledging financial achievements is a comprehensive and useful habit in the field of personal finance. It touches on motivation, introspection, thankfulness, resilience, and the joy that comes with the path to financial well-being in addition to the quantitative parts. Take time to enjoy your accomplishment, no matter how big or small—you deserve it.

CHAPTER 10: BUILDING FINANCIAL CONFIDENCE

Overcoming Financial Fears

In terms of personal finance, gaining financial well-being requires first conquering financial anxieties. Many times, having too little money can set off a range of negative emotions, including uncertainty, dread, and anxiety. It takes more than just math skills to face these anxieties head-on; you also need to be able to navigate the intricate interactions between feelings and financial realities.

A common fear is the fear of the unknown. Teens who are just beginning to navigate financial freedom may worry that they won't understand the complexities of the financial world or that they will make poor decisions. While it's important to understand that financial literacy is a journey rather than a goal, this worry is legitimate. Nobody anticipates you to know everything right away. The most important thing is to begin studying, enquiring, and getting advice.

A typical apprehension is about financial losses. The worry of encountering financial difficulties, be it an unforeseen bill, a job loss, or a downturn in the economy, may be crippling. But a strong counter to this dread is realizing that setbacks are inevitable in life and building the resilience to overcome them. Establishing an emergency fund and a financial safety net can reduce anxiety by giving people a sense of security.

The fear of debt is another common issue. It can be intimidating to think about having debt, and it's normal to be afraid of getting into a financial trap. But knowing the difference between "good" and "bad" debt, being aware of interest rates, and having a well-defined repayment strategy can all help allay this anxiety. The cure for debt anxiety is financial literacy, which enables people to make wise borrowing decisions.

Anxiety might also arise from investing for many people. Although there is a genuine fear of losing money in the market, there is also room for financial gain. Learning about various financial possibilities, diversifying a portfolio, and embracing a long-term outlook are necessary steps towards overcoming this phobia. A methodical, educated approach combined with education can turn investment anxiety into opportunity and confidence.

Financial decisions can also be influenced by fear of missing out (FOMO) on experiences and social comparison. Teens may experience peer pressure to maintain a particular lifestyle or to spend more than they can afford. It takes a strong sense of self and financial priorities to overcome this anxiety. Being aware that achieving financial success is a personal path rather than a race might help ease the anxiety associated with performing poorly in contrast to others.

In the end, conquering financial anxieties is a journey of self-awareness and empowerment. It necessitates an openness to learning, error, and adaptation. Through the use of knowledge, resilience, and a proactive mindset, people can change their relationship with money from one of anxiety to one of control and confidence. Instead of eradicating fear, the path to financial well-being is learning to face it head-on with bravery and insight.

Embracing Financial Independence

Financial independence is a thread that binds empowerment, stability, and freedom together in the fabric of life. When you're a teenager on the verge of maturity, becoming financially independent could seem far off. But the path to this important turning point starts with deliberate actions and a self-sufficiency-focused mindset.

Being financially independent is about having the freedom to make decisions that are consistent with your goals and values, not just how much money you have in the bank. It signifies the change from financial dependency to self-sufficiency, a path that entails building wealth as well as realizing how money affects your life.

To embrace financial independence, one must first develop an attitude of accountability and responsibility. It all comes down to realizing that every financial choice you make, no matter how minor, affects your future. Every decision you make, whether it's creating a budget for everyday costs or putting money aside for objectives, adds to your financial story.

The ability to responsibly handle debt is one of the pillars of financial freedom. It's critical to recognize the distinction between good and bad debt. High-interest consumer debt can prevent people from reaching financial independence, even while investments in homes or education may be deemed beneficial debt. You create the conditions for a more stable financial future by taking a disciplined approach to borrowing and debt repayment.

Another essential component of financial independence is investing. It entails using your money to work for you as well as increasing your wealth. Gaining knowledge about risk tolerance, various investment vehicles, and compound interest's power will enable you to successfully negotiate the intricate world of financial markets.

Accepting financial independence also entails being ready for unforeseen detours along the way. Creating an emergency fund offers stability and peace of mind during uncertain times by acting as a safety net for unforeseen costs. You can weather hurricanes without sacrificing your long-term financial objectives thanks to this financial buffer.

You must always be learning as you set out on the path to financial independence. The financial landscape is ever-changing, so it's important to stay up to date on market trends, shifts in the economy, and new opportunities to ensure that the decisions you make are in line with your goals.

Additionally, developing a network of mentors, financial experts, and like-minded people can offer insightful advice. You may enhance your own journey by gaining insights and tactics from people who have successfully walked the route to financial independence through sharing experiences and learning from them.

Basically, achieving financial independence is a whole-person effort. It entails developing a responsible financial mindset, making wise choices, and continuously adjusting to the changing financial environment. As you craft your story of financial freedom, keep in mind that the journey itself, the development, fortitude, and empowerment acquired along the way is just as important as the final goal. Thus, make the journey to financial freedom a rewarding and empowering experience for yourself by approaching each step with purpose.

Confidence in Your Financial Future

Upon perusing the pages of "Essential Money Skills for Teens" and assimilating the information presented, it is apparent that financial future certainty is not an ethereal objective but rather a concrete consequence of well-informed decisions and proactive decision-making.

Financial confidence is an all-encompassing feeling of empowerment and control over your financial future, not merely the capacity to manage a budget or make prudent investments. It's about realizing that, with the right use, money is a tool that can lead to a fulfilling and opportunity-filled future.

A fundamental element of sound financial management is establishing reasonable and attainable objectives. Your adolescent aspirations may include starting a small business, saving for your first car, or even paying for your college. Setting these goals early on gives you a road map that will motivate you in addition to directing your financial actions. Having a goal gives you direction and a feeling of purpose, which boosts your self-confidence and helps you write your own financial story.

You may face financial obstacles and decisions along the way that first may seem overwhelming. Every challenge, from comprehending credit scores to handling the intricacies of taxes, offers a chance to advance and develop. Even though it can be difficult at times, this learning process greatly boosts your financial confidence. Your ability to handle the intricacies of the adult financial world will improve as you master one financial topic at a time.

The capacity for shift adaptation is an essential component of financial confidence. The world of finance changes with time, and as you move through different phases of life, your objectives and ambitions could too. Gaining adaptability and flexibility in your thinking will enable you to handle these shifts with assurance. Accepting change is a sign of financial confidence, whether it's modifying your investing plan or adjusting to new banking technologies.

Creating a strong support network is another important factor in financial confidence. It can be quite beneficial to surround yourself with peers, mentors, or family members who are willing to share their financial experiences and offer advice. Gaining a wider perspective by studying the accomplishments and even failures of others gives you more confidence in your ability to make wise financial decisions.

Finally, it's critical to recognize and appreciate minor accomplishments along the route. Acknowledging and appreciating small victories, such as hitting a savings goal, sticking to a budget for a month, or choosing a wise investment, gradually boosts confidence. These instances provide concrete proof that you are mastering money rather than just learning about it.

In summary, having faith in your financial future is a journey rather than a destination. In addition to safeguarding your financial well-being, you are cultivating a lifelong attitude by embracing education, setting objectives, adjusting to change, creating a support network, and celebrating accomplishments. You can be confident that your financial future is in good hands as you finish the book's pages.

CONCLUSION

Your Financial Journey Ahead

When you come to the last pages of "Essential Money Skills for Teens," think of this as the beginning of your financial journey rather than the finish. The understanding and perceptions you've acquired from these pages are more than just lessons; they're instruments that will influence the way you relate to money going forward.

Reflecting on the Journey

It has been an adventure of learning and development for you to enter the world of financial empowerment. From comprehending the fundamentals of money to exploring the complexities of earning, saving, and budgeting, you've gained a skill set that many adults wish they had discovered sooner. Think back to the "aha" moments and epiphanies that brought notions from theoretical realms into real-world applications.

Do you recall the first time you made a budget? that turning point when you started writing your own financial story and established long-term objectives.
Acknowledge the power of financial literacy: the capacity to plan for a future that fits your goals, allocate resources sensibly, and make well-informed decisions.

The Dynamic Financial Environment

The financial sector is dynamic, changing as a result of economic upheavals, societal norm alterations, and technology breakthroughs. Your familiarity with digital payment methods, online banking, and the fundamentals of investing puts you in a position to actively participate in this changing market rather than merely observe it from a distance. Remain inquisitive and flexible; welcome the lifelong learning that comes with navigating the financial world.

The Influence of Little Actions

You have come across the power of little, steady steps throughout this book. Whether it's setting realistic financial goals, conserving a portion of your income, or carefully selecting your purchases, these seemingly small steps add up to a big difference over time. It's evidence of the compounding effect at work in investments as well as the behaviors and choices that mold your financial destiny.

Taking on obstacles head-on

Although financial difficulties are unavoidable, you'll be better prepared to handle them if you have the knowledge from these pages. You now have a toolkit of techniques to get beyond challenges and come out stronger on the other side, whether it's managing the complexities of credit and debt or knowing your obligations as a taxpayer.

Your Particular Financial Journey

At this point in time, acknowledge that your financial journey is exclusively yours. Your decisions will be guided by your values, aspirations, and goals. Accept your inner entrepreneur, look for ways to make money from your interests, and keep adjusting your budget to fit your changing priorities.

Celebrating Milestones

Celebrate all of your financial accomplishments, no matter how big or small. These accomplishments whether it's hitting a savings target, making a profitable investment, or just controlling your impulse buy are indicators of your development. Take delight in your acknowledgement of them and utilize them as inspiration for your upcoming financial actions.
An Adventure in Lifelong Learning

Being financially literate is a lifelong learning journey rather than a goal. Continue to be inquisitive and involved, and look for chances to expand your knowledge of personal finance. Recall the lessons you've learned and modify them to fit the dynamic

circumstances in your life as you take on new challenges and possibilities.
Your Financial Future Awaits

Your financial future is waiting for you with open arms as you flip the last page. Equipped with fundamental money management abilities, a financial empowerment mindset, and self-assurance to handle the intricacies of personal finance, you're in a strong position to mold a future that fits your goals. You are free to carry on with the voyage, and the options are endless.

We appreciate you taking the time to read "**Essential Money Skills for Teens**." May you have financial success, perseverance, and the ability to realize your aspirations. You have a bright future ahead of you, and the financial legacy you leave behind will be shaped by the choices you make today. Cheers to a prosperous future and the freedom to live your life as you see fit.

www.ingramcontent.com/pod-product-compliance
Lightning Source LLC
Chambersburg PA
CBHW062334290526
45794CB00005B/2034

* 9 7 9 8 8 6 9 6 3 1 8 6 2 *